SIMPLE
AF444298

Published by:

Josie Bear Publishing

ISBN 979-8-218-49700-2

Dedicated to Josie

Dear Josie,

May your faith be simple yet strong, and may you do great things that bring glory to God.

Love,
Dad

It's a simple kinda faith in this gospel,
The kind of faith where the simple seem to prosper.

And simply put it was a child
that came to save my soul.

It's a mystery to the proud and the haughty.

And when I find my self just a little lofty, I seem to miss the simple nature of this gift I own.

That GOD came down to the world He loves...

...and gave us a gift that we don't deserve.

A love so costly,
it was never free.

And He wrapped it up
and placed it on a tree,
for you and me.

"It's a simple kinda faith in this gospel. The kind of faith where a child seems to prosper, with a knowledge that the wise wish to make their own."

And you can't buy it in a store or on a website
All the money in the world could never make right.
ORNAMENTS FOR SALE
GOD BLESS!
SH

SHOP
How simply put we
are broke and need
a hand to hold.

So GOD came down to the world He loves and gave us a gift that we don't deserve...
A love so costly it was never free and He wrapped it up and hung it on a tree...

... on calvary

"It's a simple kinda faith in this gospel.
That someday soon Jesus comes with His
angels. And all the problems of this world
will melt like wax and snow."

And there are those who are part of earth's mantle, who'll rise to meet the LORD coming like a vandal, to take away the ones He loves to their proper home.

When God comes down to the world He loves and takes all the people that He calls His own. Red, yellow, tan, brown, black and white and He'll come like a thief in the night... for you and me

It's a simple kind of faith
in this gospel, the
kind of faith where
the simple seem
to prosper.

And simply put Jesus Christ came to save my soul.

About the author

Dr. Grizzly J. Proctor, a larger-than-life figure and one of the most interesting people on the planet, was born and raised in the rugged mountains, where he learned the ways of the wild and thrived off the land. Despite his unconventional upbringing, Dr. Grizzly pursued higher education and earned doctorates in Literary Arts and Theology. Known for his daring spirit, he once wrestled an alligator in Florida over a property dispute, but they have since made amends and remained close friends.

An adventurer at heart, Dr. Grizzly's life is filled with mystery and intrigue. Whether he's traversing the world or engaging in scholarly pursuits, he captivates the imagination of everyone he meets, using his unique experiences to connect with all people and foster a deep understanding of their world.

Most recently, Dr. Grizzly has ventured into the literary world with his illustrated children's book Simple, a heartwarming story that beautifully conveys the Christmas message of the birth of Jesus Christ and the overarching message of the Gospel. Based on the song "Simple" by Jeremy Michael Vess, the book reflects a desire to share timeless truths with young readers in a relatable and meaningful way.

Link for "Simple Song" download

About the artist

Link for
Barcena Art

Antonio Bárcena, a Mexican artist of international stature, is recognized for the powerful messages his works convey and the colorful contemporary style that characterizes him. "Justice, Peace, and Love" is the emblematic theme that defines his exhibitions around the world.